BOYHOODS OF GREAT COMPOSERS

THE YOUNG READER'S GUIDES TO MUSIC (I)

Boyhoods of Great Composers

by

CATHERINE GOUGH

Illustrated by
EDWARD ARDIZZONE

LONDON
OXFORD UNIVERSITY PRESS
MELBOURNE   TORONTO

Oxford University Press, Amen House, London E.C.4

GLASGOW NEW YORK TORONTO MELBOURNE WELLINGTON
BOMBAY CALCUTTA MADRAS KARACHI LAHORE DACCA
CAPE TOWN SALISBURY NAIROBI IBADAN ACCRA
KUALA LUMPUR HONG KONG

First Edition 1960
Reprinted 1961

PRINTED IN GREAT BRITAIN

INTRODUCTION

THIS BOOK tells the story of six children. They had quite different childhoods: some were rich, some were poor, some were happy and some unhappy, some had musical parents, and some had a father and mother who did not like music at all. But every one of them grew up to be a great composer, and today their music is played all over the world.

The earliest of them, Handel, was born nearly three hundred years ago. The last of them, Elgar, died less than thirty years ago. But music did not begin with Handel, and it has not ended with Elgar. Perhaps today a boy or girl is growing up who will be a great composer one day. Perhaps it is you.

LIST OF CONTENTS

Playing in the loft at night

GEORGE FREDERICK HANDEL

THREE hundred years ago Halle was one of the prettiest
towns in Germany. The houses were built of honey-
coloured stone. There were narrow streets and little
twisting alleyways, and a big market square with a tall clock-
tower in the middle. A high wall ran round the outside of the
town to keep it safe if there was a war. At that time there were
walled towns like Halle all over Germany.

One of the most important men in Halle was the chief sur-
geon. He was very good at his job; so good indeed that a duke
asked to be his patient. His name was Handel, and Frederick
was his son.

The Handels lived in a big white house in the middle of

Halle. It was called 'The Yellow Stag', and it had a great many windows. Behind it lay the ruins of another house, with a wide courtyard, and it was there that young Frederick used to go and play. He usually played by himself, as he had no brothers of his own age and only baby sisters. His parents were both very busy people, and he did not see much of them. In fact he was a rather lonely little boy.

While he was still very small his Aunt Anna came to live with the family. She quickly saw that Frederick loved music. His father and mother did not like music themselves, thinking it was a waste of time. So they were not at all pleased to hear that Frederick was musical. They refused to let him have lessons. In fact Mr Handel would not let Frederick have an instrument in the house at all, or even visit friends who owned one. He was a very strict man, and no one dared argue with him.

Aunt Anna saw that it was up to her to help Frederick learn music. The first thing to do was to find him an instrument. There were no pianos then; instead people played clavichords, which are much smaller than pianos and make a softer sound. Somehow Aunt Anna found a clavichord for Frederick to learn on. She arranged for it to be brought to the house while his father was out and put it in the loft, well out of sight. It was quite safe for Frederick to play it up there, for no one in the rest of the house could hear him. He went into the loft whenever he could and tried to teach himself to play. The best time was at night, when there was no one about to see him hurry upstairs.

Frederick now had an instrument. But Aunt Anna saw a new difficulty. She knew that he loved listening to music as well as playing it; where could she find music for him to hear? Then she thought of the big church in the square near by. Soon afterwards Mr Handel noticed that Frederick and Aunt Anna had started going to church nearly every day. As he watched them go off he told himself what a good son he had. He did not know that they really went to church to hear the organ and the choir. Frederick and Aunt Anna sat at the back of the church

With Aunt Anna in church

while the organist practised and the choir sang. Soon Frederick knew the services by heart and longed to play the organ himself.

After a time Mr Handel began to suspect something, although Frederick and Aunt Anna had been most careful not to say anything to him. He decided to send Frederick to school and see that he worked hard there. Then he would have no time even to think about music. So when Frederick was seven he went to the grammar school in Halle. The boys there had to work very long hours, mainly at Latin. But Mr Handel's plan did not succeed. The headmaster of the school himself was fond of music! Frederick was allowed to practise at school and soon became a very good player.

The following year he had an adventure which made a great change in his life. It happened like this. Frederick had a half-brother, Karl, who lived in a small town a few miles away. He was valet to the duke who ruled over the whole district. Mr Handel was the duke's doctor and visited him quite often. Frederick had never met Karl, and so one day he asked his father if he could go with him on his next visit. 'No,' said Mr Handel, 'you can't come. You're much too young.' Frederick said nothing, but once he made up his mind he never changed it. If his father would not take him in the coach, he would just have to walk all the way.

When the day came, his father set out as usual by himself. But as soon as the coach was out of sight Frederick started to follow it along the road. Luck was with him. The road was so bad that the driver was soon forced to stop the coach for repairs. Imagine the shock Mr Handel had when Frederick's face suddenly appeared at the window! He was very angry. But he could not send Frederick home by himself. So in the end he let his son climb in beside him when the coach set off again.

Karl was waiting to meet them when they arrived. He and Frederick got on very well together. In fact Frederick was such a nice, friendly boy that everyone in the palace liked him and was kind to him. He was allowed to play on the palace clavichords whenever he wanted to. He was even allowed to practise the organ in the duke's private chapel. At last he could make music without being stopped. He had never enjoyed himself so much in his life.

One day the organist actually let Frederick play a piece after the morning service. The duke himself was at the service, and stayed on afterwards to listen to the organ. When he saw Karl

The Duke talks to Mr Handel

a little later the duke told him how well the organist had been playing. 'That wasn't your organist, Your Grace,' answered Karl, 'that was my little brother Frederick!'

The duke was amazed. At once he summoned Frederick and his father. Frederick felt nervous at going to see such an important man. But really the duke wanted to talk to Mr Handel, and Frederick just sat and listened. 'Your son has a quite extraordinary talent for music,' said the duke. 'You must give him a proper training. Find a good man to teach him when you get back to Halle and see that he works hard.' Frederick's father started to argue. He told the duke that he wanted his son to be a lawyer, not a musician. Music was just something to pass the time. But the duke was firm, and Mr Handel had to give in. He did not dare to offend the great man. The duke made

Frederick and his master Zachow

him give a promise that Frederick would have music lessons. Then he took out a bag of gold coins and filled Frederick's pockets with them.

When they were back in Halle Mr Handel kept his promise. He found a very good music teacher called Zachow. Zachow saw at once that his new pupil was more musical than any boy he had ever taught. With careful training Frederick might become a great musician. So he made him work very hard, teaching him the organ and other instruments, and showing him how to write music.

At the end of three years Zachow said he had nothing more to teach him. Though he was only eleven, Frederick now played the organ and the harpsichord (an instrument rather like the piano) better than anyone else in Halle. He had also learned to write music well.

All the best music teachers were in Berlin in those days, so Frederick was sent there for a time to learn from them. While he was there, the prince who ruled Berlin heard him play. He was so impressed that he asked Mr Handel if his son could live at the royal palace, and be a court musician. But Mr Handel did not think this was a good idea at all. He still hoped that Frederick might change his mind and become a lawyer. He knew that if Frederick once started to work for the prince, he would never be able to get away again. Besides, he was very ill and wanted to see his son once more. So he wrote a letter to Berlin telling him to come home.

Frederick must have felt sad on the long, dreary journey back to Halle. There was so little music there and he did not want to be a lawyer, and now his father was ill. Soon after he got home Mr Handel died, just before Frederick's twelfth birthday. There was a big funeral, and Frederick wrote a poem in his father's memory.

Now that his father was dead, Frederick felt that he ought to follow his wishes after all. He began to work hard studying law and only played music in his spare time. There was another reason for working hard. His mother had not got much money now. She even had to give up half her house and take in lodgers. So Frederick wanted to be able to earn his living quickly, to help her.

All the same, he found time to compose some pieces of music, besides practising the organ and harpsichord. He also began to give concerts. Zachow asked friends to come and hear him play, and soon he became well known in the town. In fact people started coming from far beyond Halle to listen to him.

When he was seventeen he went to the University of Halle to study law. But only a month after the beginning of his first term a big chance came his way: the organist of Halle Cathedral had to leave suddenly, and Frederick was asked to take his place.

So at last he was able to give up the law and spend all his time on music. He did not stay in Halle much longer. After a year he went to Hamburg. Then he visited Italy. In the end he came to England and settled there. He loved London, and lived there for nearly fifty years.

He did not forget his mother and Aunt Anna, living together in the big house at Halle. Whenever he visited Germany he made a point of staying with them, however busy he was. They must have been proud to see him so famous and successful.

Apart from these trips to Germany, Frederick lived the rest of his life in England. All his best works were written there. He wrote his Water Music specially for the King of England; it was played as the royal barge sailed up the Thames. His Music for the Royal Fireworks was played during a huge fireworks display in St James's Park in London. He wrote his greatest work, *Messiah*, in London, though it was first sung in Dublin while he was on a visit there.

Today people all over the world play and sing his music. But if it had not been for Aunt Anna and the duke he might never have become a composer.

Wolfgang and Nannerl playing with their father

WOLFGANG AMADEUS MOZART

HARDLY anyone today even starts learning the piano until they are six. But by the time Wolfgang Mozart was six he already played so well that people came from far and wide to hear him. He was the most famous child player there has ever been. Later he became even more famous as a composer, and now his works are played all over the world.

Wolfgang's father was a violinist. He lived in Salzburg two hundred years ago and played in the Archbishop of Salzburg's private orchestra. Salzburg is a city in Austria. It has a big castle on a hill above the town, and there are mountains all round—you can see them in the distance whichever way you look. The Mozarts' house was in a narrow, winding street, but at the back it faced on to a broad space, where there were market stalls

B

once a week. The house is still there, and you can see the little back room where Wolfgang was born.

Wolfgang had one sister, called Marianne, or Nannerl for short. She was a very musical girl, and Mr Mozart started to teach her the clavichord when she was seven. Wolfgang was only two years old at the time, hardly more than a baby. But he used to stand beside her as she practised, and listen.

When he was three, he began to try and play on the clavichord himself. He did not simply bang the notes, like most small children, but picked out proper chords and tunes. Sometimes he even played part of the tune Nannerl had been learning. Mr Mozart was delighted to see this: Wolfgang clearly had a great gift for music. So when he was just four his father began to give him lessons too, and he and Nannerl learned together.

He quickly caught up with her. Playing scales and chords and reading music seemed to come to him naturally. When Mr Mozart began to teach him the violin he found that just as easy as the clavichord.

Soon Wolfgang even started to make up his own music. At first his father used to write this out for him. But after a short while he began to put it down on paper for himself. One day, when he was still only four, his father and a friend found him holding a piece of paper covered with ink blots. They asked him what he was doing. 'I'm writing a piano concerto,' said Wolfgang. They did not know whether to believe him, so they asked him to play it. To their surprise it really was a piece of music.

Wolfgang had very sensitive hearing and could tell if two violins were even slightly out of tune with each other. But he could not bear loud noises; for instance he hated the sound of a trumpet. At first his family thought he was only pretending not to like it. But one day, when a friend blew a trumpet close behind him, Wolfgang actually fainted! After that they believed him.

Although Wolfgang was so musical he never showed off, and in every other way he was a normal, happy boy. He was very fond of his father. When he went to bed they used to sing a little duet together; then he would kiss his father on the nose and settle down to sleep.

Mr Mozart was quite a poor man, as the Archbishop did not pay his violinists much. So when he realized how well Wolfgang and Nannerl played, he decided to arrange for them to give a public concert. People would pay to hear them, and he might earn a lot of money. At this time Wolfgang was six and Nannerl ten. He chose the nearest big city, Munich, for the concert, and there they went.

The concert was a great success. Wolfgang and Nannerl played their best, and the people of Munich were delighted by the little girl and her tiny brother. Mr Mozart was very pleased and decided to try something much bigger. They would go to Vienna, the capital of Austria, and play to the Emperor of Austria himself.

So that autumn the whole family set off for Vienna. In those days this meant a very long journey. People travelled in coaches which rattled and bumped over the rough roads. Every few miles they had to stop for fresh horses, and at night they stayed at inns on the road. There was no way to heat the coach for a winter journey or to cool it in summer. In fact travel was very uncomfortable indeed.

At last the Mozart family reached Vienna, with its wide streets, grand buildings and busy crowds. Everything there turned out as they had hoped. Almost as soon as they arrived, the Emperor invited them to play at the royal palace. He and his wife were very kind to the children, and Wolfgang and Nannerl were not at all frightened. When Wolfgang slipped and fell on the polished floor, one of the princesses helped him to his feet. He was so grateful that he asked her to marry him when they both grew

They set off for Vienna

up! The Emperor wanted to see how well Wolfgang could really play, so he gave him difficult pieces to play at sight. Then he covered the keyboard with a cloth, so that Wolfgang could not see his hands. Even so the little boy never played a wrong note.

After they had played, the Empress brought presents for them. She gave Wolfgang a grand suit, and he wore it to have his portrait painted. In this picture he looks like a little man, because children were dressed like grown-ups in those days. The suit was mauve and gold, and had a long waistcoat covered with embroidery. He wore a small white wig and carried a sword.

The visit to Vienna was a triumph for Wolfgang and Nannerl. Now that they had played to the royal family, they were famous all over Austria. Mr Mozart was delighted, but he hoped the children could do better still. There was another court he wanted to visit, even more splendid than the one in Vienna. This was the court of the King and Queen of France.

The journey was a long one, as they kept stopping on the way to give concerts. It was winter time, and the weather was cold and wet. But at last the four of them reached Paris, the French capital, just before Christmas.

Soon the King and Queen of France heard about the children, and invited them to the great palace of Versailles, just outside Paris. This palace still stands today, and it is almost as big as a small town. Now nobody lives in it, but in those days it was crowded with elegant courtiers and rich carpets and furniture.

The children noticed at once how stiff and grand everyone was. When the little princesses kissed Wolfgang and Nannerl, people looked at each other in horror.

The King was so delighted with their playing that he asked them to dinner. This was a great honour, even though they did not sit down at table. Wolfgang stood beside the Queen, and she handed him titbits from her dish as she talked to him.

After this all the wealthy and noble people in Paris asked them to come to their homes to play. This kept Wolfgang and Nannerl very busy for some time. But Mr Mozart kept thinking of new places to visit.

Beyond France lay England, where he knew the children

would get a warm welcome. The English were well-known for their kindness to foreign musicians.

So that spring the Mozarts sailed across the Channel to England. Neither Wolfgang nor Marianne had ever seen the sea before. At Calais Marianne wrote in her diary; 'How the sea runs away and comes back again!' She must have been watching big waves, which meant a rough crossing. Their little sailing ship was badly tossed about, and they were glad to reach Dover.

As soon as they arrived in London, Mr Mozart wrote to the King. He knew that King George III and Queen Charlotte loved music, and hoped they would want to hear his children play. He was right, for a letter came back asking them to the palace only five days later. The Mozarts put on their best clothes for such a grand visit.

Yet the King and Queen were so friendly that the Mozarts quite forgot they were royalty. In fact the children liked them better than all the Kings and Queens, Emperors and Empresses they had met. They were glad when they were asked back to the royal palace to play again.

One day, while they were walking in St James's Park, they heard a carriage coming near. Then the carriage window was thrown up, and a voice called out 'Hullo!' To their great surprise it was the King himself! He had known who they were even though they were now wearing their shabby old clothes.

The Mozarts had come to London to make money, so Wolfgang's father arranged a public concert as soon as he could. So many people came that there was scarcely room for them all. Wolfgang and Nannerl found it hard to believe how popular they were. After this they were asked to play at one concert after another.

But just as everything was going so well, Mr Mozart caught

a bad fever, and the doctor told him he must leave London. So the family moved to a house near Chelsea, which was a country village in those days. You can still see the house, Number 182, Ebury Street, Pimlico. The children had to be very quiet while their father was ill; the noise of their practising

Wolfgang and Nannerl meet the Queen of France

would have disturbed him. Instead, Wolfgang decided to spend the time writing music, and composed two whole symphonies.

They stayed in England for nearly a year. But at last they set off for Salzburg again. On their way through Holland both children fell seriously ill. It was several weeks before they were strong enough to go on travelling. As soon as Wolfgang could sit up in bed, he asked for a large piece of board. It was laid on the bed to make a table, and at once he started writing music.

When the Mozarts finally reached Salzburg, they had been away for nearly three and a half years, and the children were very glad to be home once more. Mr Mozart decided that Wolfgang must not travel again for a while. He needed a rest, and it was time he did some hard study. His father set him to work to write more and more difficult music.

In the attic of the Archbishop's palace

Meanwhile the Archbishop of Salzburg had heard about Wolfgang. He could not believe at first that a boy only ten years old could write good music. He thought it must be Wolfgang's father who wrote it for him. So he made Wolfgang stay at his palace for a whole week to test him. During that time, Wolfgang had to compose part of a cantata (a long piece of music for singers). No one was allowed to visit him except a servant who took him his meals. He had to sit alone in an attic, thinking and writing. At the end of the week the Archbishop came up to see what he had written. As he read the music he became more and more surprised: it was very good indeed. So the Archbishop realized that all the reports he had heard were true. He was a kindly man, and asked the students of Salzburg University to sing the cantata. On the programme was written: 'The first part of this work was set to music by Herr Wolfgang Mozart, aged ten years.'

After this success, Wolfgang had a disappointment. The family had gone to Vienna again for the marriage of the Emperor's daughter. But just before the wedding the bride caught smallpox and died. Wolfgang and Nannerl caught it too, and were very ill. When they were better, the Emperor was too sad to want to hear any music.

Wolfgang spent the next year at home in Salzburg. The Archbishop was now his friend, and made him leader of his orchestra. But his father wanted him to make one more journey, to Italy. Everyone in Italy loved music, and many composers lived there. Wolfgang could earn money by giving concerts, and also learn more about writing music.

This time Mr Mozart decided that his wife and Nannerl must stay behind. So he and Wolfgang went off on their own.

Once more everything went well. Wolfgang gave concerts and passed difficult tests. News of his fine playing went ahead of him, and everywhere great crowds came to hear him. The Mozarts reached Rome just before Easter. At this time a famous setting of the words 'Lord have mercy upon us' was always sung in the Pope's private chapel. Wolfgang was very eager to hear it, as he knew it was never sung anywhere else. He listened to the music carefully, and when he got home he wrote out what he had heard. His memory was so good that he had written down every note of it correctly.

Important people in Rome soon heard what he had done. After that the Mozarts were asked to party after party. Where-ever he played, Wolfgang was treated like a hero. Even the Pope heard about him, and later made him a knight. When they went south to Naples there were more concerts and parties. There people started saying that only by magic could a boy play so well. Perhaps it was the special ring he wore? So Wolf-gang smiled and took off his ring, and of course his playing was just as good as before.

Mr Mozart had wanted to visit Italy partly so that his son could learn more about writing operas. Wolfgang had already composed one for the Emperor of Austria, but it had never been sung in public. Now he was asked to write another, for the opera house in Milan, in Northern Italy. He worked hard and finished it in three months. He was fourteen years old when he wrote this opera.

The Italians asked him to conduct it himself. On the first night there was a great sound of cheering when he came into the orchestra pit. As the opera went on, people cheered again because it was so good. Night after night they came to hear it and to see the boy who had written it. Sometimes Mr Mozart felt so happy he wanted to cry. His son was now famous as a composer as well as a pianist.

Another writer of operas said: 'That boy will cause us all to be forgotten.' He was perfectly right, for Wolfgang was at the beginning of a great career. As he grew older, he composed more and better music, and much of it is among the finest ever written. But later in life other things did not go so well for him. He was always short of money, and often unhappy.

He must sometimes have looked back to his wonderful child-hood as the happiest time of his life.

Having a violin lesson

FRANZ SCHUBERT

WHEN Franz Schubert was a boy you could live near the middle of a big city and still be close to open country. In those days, one hundred and fifty years ago, all towns were very much smaller than they are now. The Schuberts lived in Vienna. From their house you could quickly walk to the centre of the city; the other way you were soon out among fields. Their house was easy to find, as it had a painted sign hanging out. On the sign there was a red cray-fish, and that was the name of the house. At the back of the house there was a courtyard with a garden beyond it.

Not far from the House of the Red Cray-fish was the parish

school. Franz's father was a teacher, and he was in charge of this school. When his children were old enough they started going there too. Franz's eldest brother, Ignaz, was the first to go, and next Karl and Ferdinand. Franz was the fourth boy, and he went when he was six. He had dark curly hair and a round face. He wore spectacles, which made his face look ever rounder. Everyone who met him liked Franz, because he was such a friendly boy. All through his life he had a great many friends.

All the Schubert boys were clever at something. Karl was good at drawing, and the other three boys were all musical. This was not surprising, as their father was very musical himself. But to begin with no one saw that Franz was going to be even better at music that his brothers. When Franz first went to school his father thought he was still too young to start music lessons. So, as there was a piano in the house, Franz used to go and play it by himself. When at last he began to learn music, his father found he knew a great deal already. He must have picked it up by listening to the older children and playing by himself.

When Franz was eight he started having violin lessons. His father taught him, and also showed him how to read music. Franz's father only played the violin in his spare time, but he played well enough to be able to teach it. In Vienna in those days everyone played or sang. More music was played there than in any other city in the world.

Soon his father thought Franz ought to learn the piano as well. So Franz's brother Ignaz, who was a good pianist, gave him his first piano lessons. He learnt quickly, and it was easy to see that he was very clever at music. It was not long before his father decided he was ready for a teacher outside the family. So he asked the choirmaster of the nearby church if he would give Franz singing lessons. Franz had a clear treble voice, and soon he was allowed to join the choir. His teacher was very glad to have such a good pupil. He said, 'Whenever I set out to teach him something new, I find he knows it already.' While other children have to work hard to learn music, Franz found it as easy as walking or breathing. Later on it was the same when he came to write music. Some composers have a great struggle to write down their ideas, but Franz's music came pouring out.

The Schuberts were a poor family, and had only a cheap piano. Luckily Franz made friends with a boy who was learning to be a carpenter. This boy worked in a warehouse for storing pianos, and he often let Franz come and play the good pianos that were stored there. Franz also practised on the organ at the parish church. His singing teacher was the organist, and he gave Franz organ lessons too. Franz soon played and sang very well. In fact one day his teacher asked him to play a violin solo in church. At about the same time he began to want to write music. Some people are quite happy to play and sing what others have written: Franz wanted to write his own music. His teacher showed him how to write down tunes and make up chords to go with them. Then Franz tried to write a song and a piece for the piano. But he thought they were no good, so he threw them away.

Franz was eleven now, and needed new teachers from whom he could learn more about music. The best way to find these was to win a scholarship to the royal choir. These were open to any Austrian boys who could sing really well. So Franz's parents looked carefully in their newspaper, and that summer they saw a notice about the scholarship. It said there would be an examination to choose new boys for the royal chapel in September. Any boy who wanted to try had to go to the Royal

Boarding School for tests. In order to enter for the scholarship, he had to be good at lessons as well as singing.

It was a great chance for Franz. The Royal Boarding School was the best school in Vienna. The choirboys of the royal chapel all went to the school, and were given lessons free. The

Franz is called a miller's son

headmaster loved music, and made sure that it was well taught. Franz would be able to learn how to write music properly.

Franz went to the school along with a number of other boys. When they saw him come in wearing a pale grey suit, they all started laughing. Poor Franz did not understand why, till someone called out 'miller's son'. They thought his clothes were white with flour! Many of the boys had rich parents and wore smart clothes. They turned up their noses at Franz, and no one talked to him. 'How can a funny boy with cheap clothes and spectacles hope to get into the choir?' they said to each other.

There were two examiners to choose the best from among all these boys. One of them was a very important man, as he was in charge of music at the court of the Emperor of Austria. The boys all had to pass tests in singing, playing the organ, and writing music. When it was Franz's turn to sing to the examiners, they realized at once that he had a specially good voice. Then they asked him to play and read at sight, and he did that very well too.

Soon the results were out. Three boys were to join the royal choir, and Franz was one of them. All the family were very proud of him. Term began in the late autumn, so he started getting ready. First there was all his new uniform to buy. The boys at the Royal Boarding School wore dark brown coats with a gold tab on one shoulder. They had three-cornered hats, and breeches and buckled shoes.

There were a hundred and thirty boys in the school, divided into seven groups. Each group had a room for the prefect, a study, and a dormitory. Boys came there from all over Austria. Those who lived far away only went home twice a year. Boys whose families lived in Vienna, like Franz, could go home every Sunday. Some of the boys were poor, while others were quite wealthy.

Although the school was so famous, it was not very comfortable. The class-rooms were cold, and the boys had long waits between meals. They used to spend most of their pocket money on fruit and buns. In fact Franz wrote a letter to Ferdinand saying: 'As you know, we all like to eat a roll or a few apples sometimes, and all the more so if, after a poor lunch, we have to wait eight and a half hours for a miserable evening meal.' He hoped his brother would send him some money to pay for more food.

Franz was happy at the school in spite of this. As usual, he quickly made friends. He also got on well with his work. His reports have been kept, and he got good marks in all subjects. As you would expect, he got the highest marks for music. 'A special talent for music' the master wrote at the end of one report.

There was a music practice room in the school, and Franz went there every day. Soon other boys started going to listen to him. Franz made up tunes for them, and sang them his own songs. He wrote down one song and a piano duet the first year he was at the school. As a choirboy, Franz knew all about singing, and he wrote more and more songs. He would find a poem, and then try to write music to go with it. Sometimes he thought of a song very suddenly. If he was out at a café, he wrote the music on a menu!

All the boys who came to the practice room were his friends. They had great fun together, singing and listening. But they did not all know that Franz wrote down his songs. He told only one boy, his special friend Josef. Josef was much older than Franz, but they became very good friends. One day Franz told Josef that he had used up all his music paper, and had no money to buy any more. So Josef bought him a huge pile of paper, enought to write down dozens of songs.

There was a school orchestra, and Franz played the violin in it. Because he played so well he was soon made first violin and led the orchestra. Sometimes, if the conductor was away, Franz took his place. The orchestra had not been started very long when Franz joined it, but each term its playing grew better. In the summer they played in a room with all the windows open. People passing in the Square below stopped to listen to them.

Franz also played music at home, on Sundays and in the holidays. In fact the Schuberts had a family quartet. Ignaz and Ferdinand played the violins, Franz the viola, and his father the cello.

The family quartet

If you can play the violin, it is quite easy to play the viola too. It is a little larger than the violin, and you can play lower notes on it. Friends came to listen to the Schubert quartet, and it was famous in their part of Vienna.

Franz was learning to write music for quartets now, and also for orchestras. He took home each new piece for the family to play. The man who taught him was one of the two men who had examined him. He was in charge of music at the Emperor's

c

court, and hardly ever gave lessons to schoolboys. Because it was such an honour to be taught by this man, Franz was allowed to break a school rule. This said that no boy at the Royal Boarding School could ever go out alone. But the headmaster let Franz go by himself to his music lessons twice a week.

The choirboys had to do well at other subjects besides music, but now Franz wanted to spend all his time playing and writing tunes. He began to fall a little behind with some of his lessons. This did not matter while he sang in the choir, but when he was fifteen his voice broke. He could no longer sing treble, and he could only stay on at the school if he did well at all his lessons. The headmaster told Franz he must work specially hard for a year; his father also urged him to spend less time on music. He did not think Franz would ever earn much money as a musician, and wanted him to be a schoolmaster instead.

But Franz found it difficult to work at other things when there was so much music going on. Sometimes he and a friend spent an evening at the opera. Once he sold some school books to pay for a ticket to an opera he specially wanted to hear. There were a great many concerts to go to as well. And all the time he was writing more and more music. In the year he left the choir he wrote his first symphony, and the school orchestra played it.

This did not leave him much time for his other lessons, and at the end of the year he was made to leave the school. He must have been sad to leave when he was only sixteen, but he often went back. For one thing, he went on playing in the school orchestra. He also met his friends there, and played them his latest music.

After he had left school, Franz earned his living for a few years by teaching. But he spent all his spare time writing music and playing it with his friends. In the year after he started teaching he wrote one hundred and fifty songs. He grew up to be the greatest song writer there has ever been. When a singer gives a concert today he usually sings one of Schubert's songs. He wrote a great many other kinds of music as well. His symphonies are very much loved, and so is his music for piano and

Franz sings for his friends

for quartets. His most famous work is the Unfinished Symphony, which is only half the length of a complete symphony. (There was no particular reason why he did not finish it—he just put it on one side halfway through and never came back to it.)

Franz Schubert wrote music more quickly than almost any other composer. Not even Mozart wrote faster than he did. This was just as well, because he did not have a long life: he died when he was only thirty-two. By then he had already written as much as other men write in a complete lifetime.

He always had a great many friends. They often listened to him playing or singing, at home or in cafés. And many of these friends had been boys with him at the Royal Boarding School. It was there, too, in the royal choir that he learnt all about singing. Without that training he could never have written such wonderful songs. So perhaps the most important day in his life was the day he was chosen to be a royal choirboy. The other boys had laughed at him in his funny clothes, but he was to become more famous than any of them.

The Mendelssohns' house in Berlin

FELIX MENDELSSOHN

THE Mendelssohns were very rich indeed. They lived nearly a hundred and fifty years ago in an enormous house in Berlin, with a large garden and many servants. They were also clever and artistic. Felix's mother and father were very fond of music, and their four children could all play or sing. Felix played the violin and the piano, and so did his sister Fanny; their younger brother Paul played the cello, and Rebecca, the youngest, was good at singing.

It was a great help to Felix to belong to such a family. Because his parents loved music themselves, they helped him to learn how to play and compose. Because they were also very rich, he never had to worry about money. 'Felix' means 'lucky' in Latin, and indeed he seems to have been lucky in every way.

As soon as the children could play well enough, the family started giving concerts at home. They gave a concert almost every Sunday morning until the children grew up. Often grown-up players joined in too, and friends came to listen. If many people came, they would play in a large summer house so that there was room for everyone. This stood in the middle of the big garden behind the Mendelssohns' house. Otherwise they all sat round the big table in the dining-room.

Although all the children were musical, Felix and Fanny played even better than the other two. Fanny was four years older than Felix, but they were always close friends. They also started to learn music at the same time. Their mother could play the piano, and she gave them their first lessons. To begin with they only played for five minutes a day, but soon the lessons grew longer. Their mother took a great interest in their musical training. Even when the children went to another teacher later on, she still sat beside them while they practised, doing her knitting.

When Felix was seven, his father had to go to Paris on business. He was a banker, and often had to go abroad. This time he decided to take Felix and Fanny with him. But he was afraid they might get bored while he was busy all day, so he found a piano teacher and asked her to give them lessons. Felix and Fanny liked her, and got on very well. In fact they got on so well that their father decided they should have proper music teachers when they got home again.

So when they came back to Berlin, he arranged for them to have lessons on the piano and the violin, and to learn how to write music. They already worked hard at their ordinary lessons, and so this meant that their days were very full indeed. Every morning except Sunday they had to get up and start work at five o'clock. There was a short break for lunch. But if Felix stayed on and chatted after the meal was over his mother would say: 'Felix, are you doing nothing?' and send him back to his lessons.

When work was over for the day the children played in the garden. The Mendelssohns' garden was so big that it was more like a park. There were lawns and avenues, and even a small wood. This was lucky for Felix, as he loved climbing trees. He was a very lively boy, and working hard did not tire him. He was also good-looking, with thick curly hair and rosy cheeks. Everyone who met him liked him, because he was so gay and friendly. He was eager to learn about new things and meet new people.

Felix learned music quickly, and was soon very good at the piano and the violin. As the Mendelssohns had plenty of money, he did not need to play in public. He and Fanny never went on concert tours like Wolfgang and Marianne Mozart. But when Felix was nine, his father thought it would not hurt him to play at one real concert. He did so, and everyone thought he played very well. But his father was glad to see that the success did not go to Felix's head. He did not want his son to grow up too pleased with himself, and he was always very strict. Felix was not allowed to play in public again for another three years.

By the time he was eleven he was ready to start writing music as well as playing it. At first he was too small to work at a big table, so he sat on a footstool and wrote on his knee. One day a friend found him sitting there, writing busily. He asked Felix what he was doing, and was told he was composing a quartet.

This is a work for four instruments, a difficult thing for a boy to write. But Felix's quartet was so good that it was actually printed. Soon he was composing pieces for more instruments, and even for a whole orchestra.

Sometimes Felix's works were played at the family's Sunday morning concerts. He used to conduct them himself, standing

Felix writing music

on a chair. Afterwards the family would discuss the piece. They told him which parts of it were good and which were bad. Then he would go away and alter it to make it sound better.

At about the same time he started writing songs. By now he was going to the famous Singing School in Berlin. But Fanny still had music lessons with him at home, and she started writing songs too. In fact she learned to play and write almost as well as Felix, but her father would not let her make music her career.

After a short time Felix tried to write something far more difficult than a song. This was an opera, for many singers and an orchestra as well. He had just met a famous composer of operas called Weber, and was very excited by his music. Soon afterwards a friend of Weber's came to the Mendelssohns' house. Felix was eager to hear one of Weber's operas, so he asked the friend to play it to him on the piano. It took nearly three hours, but Felix listened carefully the whole time. Three days later he was able to play the complete opera himself from memory.

All Felix's teachers were proud of him, but especially the man who taught him how to write music. His name was Zelter, and he was a friend of the great German poet Goethe. The poet was an old man now, and Zelter thought he would enjoy meeting a clever and friendly boy like Felix. So when Felix was twelve he and Zelter set off to visit Goethe's home, which was a long way from Berlin. The Mendelssohn family were very anxious that Goethe should like Felix, and told him to behave nicely. His father reminded him to speak clearly and to remember his manners at table.

Goethe was walking in his garden when Felix and Zelter arrived. He gave them a warm welcome, and wanted to hear how Felix played and what he thought about music. First he gave him a piece by Beethoven. It had never been printed and was untidy and covered with blots. Even so, Felix was able to play it correctly. Then Goethe asked him to play the piano, making up the music as he went along. So Felix went to the piano and began. He started off with loud chords and then went on to play fast and exciting music. It was such a wild piece that Goethe asked 'What goblins and dragons have you been dreaming about to drive you along so wildly?' Goethe liked Felix so much that he asked him to stay for a fortnight, and till the end of his life they remained good friends.

Next year Felix went even further away from home. His family decided that they would all go to Switzerland for a holiday, travelling in carriages. They stopped at various places

Meeting Goethe in the garden

on the way. One morning, not long after they had started out, they suddenly noticed that Felix had got left behind. There was a panic, and his tutor set off to find him. Soon he met Felix, happily walking through the fields to catch up with them. He had asked a village girl to show him the way, and was not in the least afraid of being lost.

Felix was now thirteen and beginning to wear grown-up clothes. Up till then his curly hair had reached his shoulders,

but now it was cut short.
At the same time his music
teacher told him that
as a musician he was
now grown up. Felix
had just written an
opera, and it was
being sung in a
theatre in Berlin. It
was so good that his
teacher said afterwards,
'My dear boy, from this

Felix at thirteen

day you are no longer a learner, but a full member of the
brotherhood of musicians.'

But sometimes Felix still felt shy like an ordinary child. A
famous pianist visited Berlin, and came to supper with the
Mendelssohns. Afterwards Felix was asked to play, but he felt
so nervous that he burst into tears and ran from the room. In
spite of this, the pianist offered to give him lessons. This was
because he had heard from other people how well Felix played.

Although Felix was so good at both writing and playing
music, his father could not make up his mind: should he allow
Felix to make music his career, or not? He wanted another
man's opinion, and thought of the composer Cherubini. He
had to go to Paris again on business, and that was where Cherubini lived. So Felix set off for Paris with his father soon after his
sixteenth birthday. They both knew that Cherubini was hard
to please; if he thought Felix was good, it was real proof that
the boy was a fine musician.

Usually Cherubini was gruff, but he spoke kindly to Felix.
He listened to several of Felix's pieces and looked at a few others.

Then he told Mr Mendelssohn that his son would certainly be a good composer, and so the question was settled. The Mendelssohns stayed in Paris till May, and Felix met some other well-known composers. But he did not like French music at all. He thought it was not serious enough, and liked German music much better.

Felix's school days were now nearly over. When he was seventeen he became a student at Berlin University, and in the same year he wrote what is probably his most famous piece of music. It is the music to be played before Shakespeare's play *A Midsummer Night's Dream*, and it is delightful to hear. As you listen to the quick, light music, you cannot help seeing the fairies dancing in the woods. Later there are some loud notes which sound like a donkey braying. These make you think of the man who is turned into a donkey in the play. In fact the music follows the play very closely. Felix and Fanny had been reading the play together just before he wrote it. This *A Midsummer Night's Dream* music was first played at a concert in the open air, and that is the best way to hear it.

When he was grown up, Felix wrote much fine music, but his best pieces were mostly written when he was a young man. He married and had children, and many successes came his way. His life was almost always happy, though he died quite young, and everyone loved his music. Yet not many of his later works are played today. Perhaps he wrote best when he was at home with the family, conducting his music in the big summer house.

On the quay at Bergen

EDWARD GRIEG

I F you draw a line from the Shetland Islands, to the north of Scotland, across the North Sea, it comes to the town of Bergen in Norway. Bergen is a fishing port, with a big harbour full of boats. You can see the masts showing above the roofs from every part of the town. Down on the quay the fishermen spread out their nets to dry. Close by is the fish market. The whole town smells of the sea, and tar, and fish.

Two hundred years ago a man sailed across the North Sea to Bergen from Scotland. His name was Alexander Greig. He liked Bergen, and made up his mind to settle there. But he found that the Norwegians all said his name wrong. So he changed Greig to Grieg, and then they said it the right way.

Alexander Grieg began sending lobsters to Scotland for people to eat. It was not long before he became rich, and the family moved into a big house. Soon the Griegs felt they were Norwegians rather than Scotsmen. Alexander's son and grandson both married Norwegian girls.

This grandson (another Alexander) was the father of the composer. He too lived in Bergen, and he carried on the family business. Both he and his wife were fond of music. Alexander could not play himself, but his wife was a fine pianist. She even took part in concerts in Bergen.

After they were married they set up house near the harbour. They had five children, three daughters and two sons. Edward was the younger of the two boys. He was born a little over a hundred years ago. He had large blue eyes and thick fair hair, and was a dreamy-looking little boy.

Edward loved looking at the boats in the harbour. He used to walk along the quays among the nets and the baskets of fish. Often he watched the boats put out to sea and vanish beyond the horizon. If the weather was wet, he had to stay indoors instead. One rainy day he thought he would like to try and play the piano. He started by playing one note, and then another with it to make a chord. All the time he listened very carefully to the sound. At first he only played with one hand. Then he found he got a richer sound by using both hands together.

His mother was very glad to hear him playing. Because she loved music so much, she had always hoped that her children would be musical. When he was six she decided he was old enough for piano lessons. She taught him herself. She was a strict and careful teacher. Edward had to practise a great many scales and exercises each day. He found these boring and used to hurry over them; it was much more fun to play tunes. But he knew his mother always listened while he practised. She used to call out from the kitchen when he played a wrong note.

Once a week friends came to the Griegs' house to play and sing together. There were very few concerts in Bergen, so people had to make their own music. Edward's mother played the piano at these musical evenings. Edward was too young to join in, but he sat in a corner and listened. He heard a great deal of music in this way.

When Edward was nine his grandfather died. The old man had been very important in the town, so he had a big funeral. His parents took Edward to it. An army band played a special march, and Edward found the slow, sad music very moving. In fact he remembered it for the rest of his life.

Later that year the Griegs moved into a house that had belonged to Edward's grandfather: it was a large house out in the country near Bergen. The garden was very big, and there was a drive up to the front door. The boys had a long walk to school in Bergen each day.

Edward did not enjoy school at all. He found the lessons dull and he hated the masters. The school was very strict, and he was always getting into trouble. This was because he never liked keeping rules. But he found a clever way of avoiding school. It rains a great deal in Bergen, and Edward was often soaked through when he reached school. Then the teacher sent him home again to change his clothes. So when it only rained a little bit, Edward went and stood under a rain-spout to get really wet. But he was caught in the end: one day when it was hardly raining a master found out what he done. So he would not play that trick any longer!

Meanwhile Edward's mother made him work hard at the piano. By now he could play well, and he began to want to write music also, as his head was full of tunes. One day he sat at his desk and wrote at the top of a piece of paper: 'Variations on a German tune by Edward Grieg, Opus 1'. Then he wrote his music underneath. He took it to school and showed it to a friend. During the class, the teacher saw that this boy was saying something. So he asked him to speak louder.

'Grieg has something,' muttered the boy.

'What do you mean, Grieg has something?' asked the teacher.

'Grieg has composed something!'

So Edward had to show the teacher what he had written. The teacher looked at it, and called the master from the next class to see it as well. Edward watched them eagerly, hoping they would like it. The two teachers looked carefully at the sheet of paper. But as soon as the other master had gone, Edward's own teacher lifted him up by his hair. 'Get on with your work and leave such trash at home!' he shouted. Edward was bitterly disappointed.

But he found at least one friend who liked his music. This was a young soldier who lived near the school. He was very musical, and played the piano well. Edward often went to visit him after school. He showed the soldier what he had written, and always got helpful advice.

All the same, Edward did not think he was good enough at music to make it a career. If people asked him what he wanted to be, he always answered 'a clergyman'. He used to pretend that a chair was his pulpit and stood behind it as if he was preaching. But instead of a sermon he used to say poems. In fact he loved poetry almost as much as music, and learnt a great many poems off by heart. He always made the family listen to him; it was no fun saying the poems with nobody there. Sometimes his father almost fell asleep in his chair while Edward recited. When he got to the end, his father wanted him to stop, but Edward always called out, 'Oh, just one little piece more.'

It was a long time before Edward thought he could be a musician when he grew up. At last a man called Ole Bull made

'Leave such trash at home!' he shouted

up his mind for him. Ole Bull was a great Norwegian violinist who had played all over the world. He bought a house near the Griegs, and promised to visit them. Edward was very excited. He knew all about him, and felt that a real hero was coming to the house.

Edward stood watching by the door on the day of the visit. He saw Ole Bull come galloping on horse-back up the long drive. Then he went forward to meet him, and they shook

D

hands. Edward was so excited that he felt as if an electric shock had gone through him. He could hardly believe his eyes when he saw Ole Bull walk into the house and greet his mother just like any other man.

Edward's parents told Ole Bull that their son was musical. So the great violinist asked if Edward would play to him.

The arrival of Ole Bull

Edward played several pieces that he had written himself. Then he was sent out of the room while Ole Bull talked to his parents.

After a while Ole Bull came out to him and said, 'You are to go to Leipzig and become a musician.' So at last Edward knew that his music was good enough. Ole Bull himself thought he should make it his career. His parents agreed, and it was all settled very quickly.

They decided to send him to Leipzig, in Germany, because

that was the best place in Europe to learn music. There was no
school of music in Norway. Mendelssohn had started the one
at Leipzig, and now people went there from many countries.

Edward was very young to go all that way by himself.
Luckily a friend of his father's was going to Germany, so
Edward went with him. He was still only fifteen, and felt very
homesick. Leipzig was quite
different from Bergen. It was
far inland and the streets
were dark and narrow.
It seemed to Edward
to be a very old and
shabby town.

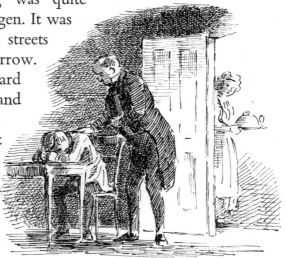

When he first got
there, he sat in his
bedroom and
cried to be home
in Norway. The
landlord found
him there when
he came to tell

But Edward went on crying

him that dinner was ready. 'See, my dear Mr Grieg,' he said, 'we
have the same sun, the same moon, and the same God here that
you have at home.' But Edward went on crying.

After a short time he settled down and started studying. At
first the other students treated him like a child, because he
looked so young in his Norwegian blouse with a leather belt.
One of them made him angry by taking him on his knee for
fun, just as if he really was a child. But after a time he made a
number of friends.

Edward had looked forward to the music lessons at Leipzig.

He thought that at the end of three years there he would know everything about music. But soon he was disappointed. The work was often difficult, and some of the teachers were dull. He hated learning all the hard rules for writing music. He wanted to write it straight away, anyhow, as it came into his head.

But in spite of his grumbles he worked hard, and learnt a great deal. He visited several other countries after he had finished at Leipzig, and then went back to Norway a very well trained musician.

For several years he taught music and arranged concerts in order to make enough money to live on. Later he was able to build a house in the country and spend all his time writing music. People began to see that he was Norway's greatest composer. He wrote music for the piano and for orchestras, and many songs. The most famous of his works are the Peer Gynt Suite and the piano concerto. He also spent much time looking for old songs and dances and arranging them for people to play and sing. By doing this he hoped to show the people of Norway how much lovely music there already was in their country.

All his life Grieg loved Norway, and was never happy when he was away from it. He liked best to be among the mountains or by the sea. For it was the sea and the mountains which gave him the ideas for his greatest music. He was specially fond of Bergen, and often went back there in later years. If Alexander Greig had not decided to settle in Bergen so many years before, perhaps Norway would never have had a great composer.

Mr Elgar's music shop

EDWARD ELGAR

To Edward Elgar, playing a musical instrument was as natural as eating or sleeping. Music-making went on all day in the Elgars' house, and everyone in the family loved it. Luckily they lived in a town where there was plenty of music. This was Worcester, which is an English cathedral city. All cathedrals have lovely singing and playing, but Worcester had more music still. Once a year the choir joined with the choirs of two other cathedrals to sing together. They still do this, and it is called the Three Choirs Festival.

Worcester is also a pleasant place to live in because of the beautiful country around it. The river Severn runs close beside the cathedral. From the city you can look across to the steep line of the Malvern Hills, and everything is green and peaceful. Edward Elgar was always very fond of the Worcester countryside. Many years later, when he came to live in London, he called his home Severn House.

Edward's father, William Elgar, was born in London, and there he learned to make and tune pianos. When he was fully trained he made up his mind to start his own business. So he went to Worcester and opened a music shop. (He also got a job as an organist at a nearby church.) Then he had a stroke of luck. King William IV died, and his widow went to live near Worcester. Her name was Queen Adelaide. She liked music, and when she left London she took her piano with her. She needed someone to tune it and asked William Elgar if he would do so. In this way he became the royal piano tuner. Now he got plenty of other customers as well. He soon found he had enough money to buy a house and get married.

William and his wife had seven children. The three eldest were born in Worcester, and then their parents decided to move to the country. They found a pretty cottage called 'The Firs' at Broadheath. This is a village beside a big common a few miles from Worcester. Edward was born here, just over a hundred years ago, and so were three more children. Later they had to move back to Worcester, but the children went on coming to a farm at Broadheath for holidays.

When they went back to Worcester their new home was opposite the cathedral. This was in the High Street, the busiest part of the town. It was noisy and crowded, with lots of twisting, narrow streets nearby. The children loved exploring every corner and alleyway. The shop was on the ground floor, and the family lived over it. But the two parts of the house were not really separate. The family sitting-room was at the back on the ground floor, and there was a show-room on the floor above. So the children spent a lot of their time in the shop. You could buy instruments there as well as printed music. There were violins and oboes and flutes in the window and out on the counter. You could also have music lessons at the shop, because Mr Elgar taught the violin. All day long music was being played somewhere in the house.

The Elgar children were all musical, and at first no one thought Edward was better than the others. In fact his brother Joe seemed to be the best. The family even nicknamed him 'Beethoven'. But he died when he was only seven, at the same time as a sister did. So that left five children.

From as far back as he could remember Edward had watched people play and sing. But when he was five he noticed that they always had pieces of music in front of them. When he looked at these sheets of music he saw that they all had lines drawn on them. So he made up his mind to make some music of his own. He went out by himself, sat down on the doorstep, and started ruling lines on a piece of paper. Nearby a man was painting a house. He was interested to see Edward drawing there, and soon came down his ladder to see what he was doing. He looked over the boy's shoulder and saw the lines all neatly ruled. But the number was wrong! And so it was a painter who first taught Edward to write his music on five lines, not four.

Soon after this Edward went to his first school. One of the teachers gave piano lessons, and he started to learn with her. But it was the violin that he really wanted to learn. He begged to have lessons, and in the end his father let him. Even this did not satisfy Edward, and he started teaching himself other instruments also. In his father's shop he could choose what instruments he liked. He taught himself to play the bassoon well, and also the viola and cello. When he came to write music he found it a great help to know all these instruments.

Edward started trying to compose when he was ten. It seemed to him a natural thing to do; after all his father often wrote pieces for the choir to sing at the church where he was

Edward's first lesson in writing music

organist. Once Edward and his father were sheltering from the rain. Edward watched his father take out a notebook and quickly write down a tune. It had just come into his head, and he wanted to write it down before he forgot it.

So Edward went about with a notebook too. One day the family found him sitting by the river with his notebook open. They asked him what he was doing. He said he was trying to write down the music the reeds were making. Nobody knows if he really wrote any notes that time, but he did soon afterwards. The children made up a play while they were on holiday at Broadheath. Edward offered to write some music to go with it. Their play was all about a magic land beyond the stream at the bottom of the garden. No grown-ups were ever allowed to go into it. Edward wanted to have some low notes in his music, but he had nothing to play them on. So he made a kind of bass violin specially for the play.

Edward was used to watching his father play music as well as write it. He went to church with Mr Elgar on Sundays and watched him play the organ. In fact Edward was so fond of church music that he actually ran to hear it every week. First he went to his father's church, then he raced down High Street for the last part of the cathedral service. It was not long before he wanted to play the organ himself. His father gave him some lessons, and Edward found a book to help him. Soon he was good enough to play hymns at a service.

Edward spent a lot of time in his father's shop, looking through the piles of music for nice pieces to play. When he first wanted to write music he found dozens of books there on how to compose, and he read through them steadily. He did all the exercises they set, and in this way gave himself a good musical training.

He was a great reader, too. But the house was so full and busy that it was hard to find a quiet place. So he started getting up two hours before the rest of the family in order to read in peace. When he read plays, he enjoyed saying parts of them out loud. A man called Ned who had once been an actor worked in the music shop. He told Edward all about the theatre, and taught him to say long pieces from Shakespeare's plays. One day a neighbour complained to Mrs Elgar that she had heard

Edward swearing. But his mother answered that he was only reciting poetry!

When he was eleven he went to a new school called Littleton House. The headmaster was very friendly and kind, and so Edward liked the school and did well. He had a good memory, and never bothered to learn his homework till he was on the

At the Glee Club

way to school. He was very serious at this time, and also very thin. For his last two terms at the school he was head boy.

By the time he went to Littleton House Edward could play the violin quite well. His father decided that it was time he joined the Worcester Glee Club. This was a group of men who met every week to sing and play and chat. They all sat at long tables by candlelight. Then they lit their pipes and were given mugs of ale. Edward was only ten when he first went, but he was allowed to smoke! If it was an evening for playing, not singing, they all had to put down their pipes. Edward got useful practice at the Glee Club playing the violin with other people, and he heard much new music.

All this time he enjoyed music and was very keen to learn new instruments. But he had never yet been really thrilled by it. Then one day he was reading through music in his father's shop, as he often did. This time he started looking at Beethoven's First Symphony. He glanced through the first part, and thought it was not very interesting. Then he came to the fast third movement. As he looked at the notes he suddenly became very excited. He ran out of the house in order to find a quiet place, and then he opened the book again. Full of wonder, he tried to sing the piece through in his head. Never in his life had he come across such wonderful music; it was richer than anything he had ever seen or heard before.

Now Edward was sure he wanted to make music his career. He decided to go to Leipzig to study, like Grieg. At that time it was still the best place in Europe to learn music. So he started learning German while he was still at school. But there was a disappointment waiting for him: his father could not possibly afford to send him to Leipzig. The music shop did not make much money, and Mr Elgar had four other children to provide for. In fact Edward now had to start earning his own living, although he was only fifteen.

His parents wondered what career he should take up. They thought he would make a good lawyer because he was such a serious, hard-working boy, and so a friend of his father's offered to take him into his office. Edward went there and did his best to work hard. But all the time his heart was set on becoming a musician. He kept in practice by playing the violin and helping his father with the organ. At last his father saw that Edward was not really happy learning to be a lawyer. He needed help in the shop, so he asked Edward to join him. At the same time, Edward became assistant organist to his father.

Already there was one branch of music in which he was better than his father. This was playing the violin. Soon he started playing at concerts and giving lessons all over Worcester. In fact he became well known as a violinist before people knew he was a composer.

The piles of music paper grew in his room

But all this time he went on teaching himself to write music better. The piles of music paper grew in his room as he waded through book after book of musical exercises. He also read and listened to all the music he could. If ever an opera company visited Worcester, he went to hear them. He played in more than one orchestra, and got to know a great many pieces in that way. In fact he took advantage of every chance that came to him.

He had to work for years before he could write music that people liked. He had many disappointments, and for a long time was short of money. But at last, quite suddenly, people realized that he was a great composer.

They heaped honours on him. He was made a knight, and given a rare decoration called the Order of Merit. All over England his music was played and loved. Not for two hundred years had an Englishman written such good music. He wrote symphonies, concertos, pieces for choirs, and many other things. His most famous work for orchestra is called the 'Enigma' Variations. In this he made musical pictures of his friends at Worcester. 'Enigma' means 'puzzle', but no one quite knows what the puzzle is, or even if there is one at all—Edward was fond of practical jokes! His 'Pomp and Circumstance' Marches are also well known (the tune of 'Land of Hope and Glory' comes from one of these).

People once called England the 'land without music'. It was Edward Elgar who first proved them wrong. Since his time there have been several great English composers. But it was his example which encouraged them. We owe a lot to Mr Elgar's music shop in Worcester.

PRINTED IN GREAT BRITAIN
BY RICHARD CLAY AND COMPANY, LTD.,
BUNGAY, SUFFOLK

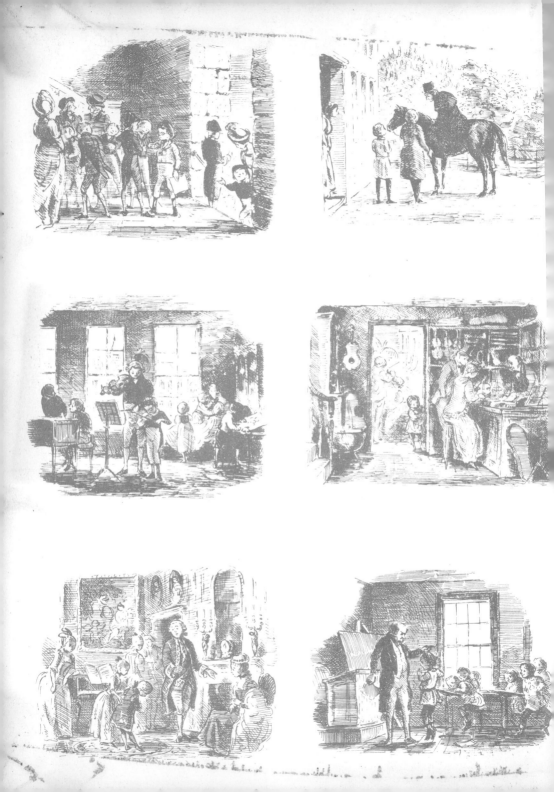